THE AMERICAN POETRY REVIEW/HONICKMAN
FIRST BOOK PRIZE

The Honickman Foundation is dedicated to the support of projects that promote spiritual growth and creativity, education and social change. At the heart of the mission of the Honickman Foundation is the belief that creativity enriches contemporary society because the arts are powerful tools for enlightenment, equity and empowerment, and must be encouraged to effect social change as well as personal growth. A current focus is on the particular power of photography and poetry to reflect and interpret reality, and, hence, to illuminate all that is true.

The annual American Poetry Review/Honickman First Book Prize offers publication of a book of poems, a $3,000 award, and distribution by Copper Canyon Press through Consortium. Each year a distinguished poet is chosen to judge the prize and write an introduction to the winning book. The purpose of the prize is to encourage excellence in poetry, and to provide a wide readership for a deserving first book of poems. *All-American Poem* is the eleventh book in the series.

All-American Poem

All-American Poem

Matthew Dickman

Winner of the APR/Honickman First Book Prize

The American Poetry Review
Philadelphia

Distribution by Copper Canyon Press/Consortium.

Library of Congress Control Number: 2008925017

ISBN 978-0-9776395-6-4 (cloth, alk. paper)
ISBN 978-0-9776395-4-0 (pbk., alk. paper)

FIRST EDITION

Designed by Valerie Brewster

for Michael, Mike, and Carl

Contents

Part Three

Acknowledgments

Thank you to the editors of the following magazines where some of these poems first appeared:

American Poetry Review: "The Cows of Point Reyes," "The Mysterious Human Heart," "Roma"

Asheville Poetry Review (Jazz Issue): "Chick Corea is Alive and Well!"

Boston Review: "Lents District," "Country Music"

Lyric: "We Are Not Temples," "American Studies"

Missouri Review: "Public Parks," "Slow Dance," "Classical Poem," "The Small Clasp"

Narrative: "Some Days," "All-American Poem"

The New Yorker: "Grief," "Trouble"

The following poems have also appeared in the chapbook *AMIGOS* published by Q Ave Press, 2007, edited by Sebastian Matthews: "Amigos," "American Studies," "Byron Loves Me," "Classical Poem," "Grief," "Love," "Public Parks," "The Black Album," "Slow Dance."

"The Mysterious Human Heart" is for David Grubin

"The Black Album" is for Major Jackson

"The Cows of Point Reyes" is for Laura Murphy

I am grateful to so many who were a part of this book including Carl Adamshick, Mike McGriff, Jillian Weise, Major Jackson, Ernie Casciato (my sergo), Andrea, Isamu, and Gilbert Nakayama, Jessie Sue Hibbs (my constant correspondent), Laura Murphy, my poetry parents Dorianne Laux and Joe Millar, Marie Howe, Preston Mark Stone, Jessica Grindell, Ingrid Powell, Charles Seluzicki, David Rivard, Alan Shapiro, Joan and David Grubin, Sebastian Matthews, Camille Dungy, Britta

Ameel, Khaled Mattawa, Paul Yoon, Kate Dempsey, Crystal Williams, Naomi Shihab Nye, Matthew Lippman, my Greater Trumps Cliff, Hope, Janice, Karla, Joe, Jolie and Javid, The Vermont Studio Center in Johnsonville, Vermont, The Michener Center for Writers in Austin, Texas, and The Fine Arts Work Center in Provincetown, Massachusetts.

Thank you to Elizabeth Scanlon for her immense spirit, detailed attention to this collection, and for showing me The Moon Tree.

Thank you to Tony Hoagland for his eyes, ears, dervish-heart and humongous soul.

Thank you to APR, The Honickman Foundation, and Copper Canyon Press.

And especially to my family: Michael Dickman, Elizabeth Dickman, Frances Cobb, The Castelluccis, Dana Huddleston, Darin Hull, and my mother Wendy Dickman, for all their love, support, and celebration of poetry.

Introduction

I feel fortunate to be the one to introduce Matthew Dickman's big, wacky, humane poems to the world of readers. No great persuasive powers are required, since the poems are about as athletic and winsome as a giant American spaniel at the beach— jumping into the water, chasing the Frisbee, digging a hole to China, burying your cell phone. As Frank O'Hara once suggested, the writing of a poem might be a very reasonable substitute for the average phone call—he would be sure of it now.

Matthew Dickman's all-American poems are the epitome of the pleasure principle; as clever as they are, they refuse to have ulterior intellectual pretensions; really, I think, they are spiritual in character—free and easy and unself-conscious, lusty, full of sensuous aspiration, tarted up in metaphor, getting Cirque du Soleil fingerpaints on everything. We turn loose such poets into our culture so that they can provoke the rest of us into saying everything on our minds. They use the bribery of imagination to convince us of the benefits of liberty.

In a poem like "Snow," for instance, the poet can begin in a manner as charmingly naïve as this:

> Let's put on our gloves and scarves
> and walk out under the birches
> into the white world!

Which then pivots unobtrusively into a slightly more subversive insinuation:

> We can make snow angels with Rockefeller and most
> of Harvard Law. The white world I'm talking about.

A few lines later the poem has stoked-up to cruising velocity, into Kerouacian riffs which whirl out their baroque pleasures:

> ...Santa is somewhere in red leather
> smoking a pipe that smells like cinnamon.

He is Christmas white the way Jesus is, sleeping
in a cradle in Palo Alto
below the twinkling lights of a Starbucks
where candy cane mochas
are flying out the window like geese
out of hell. It is fucking co-old
out here. The big flakes coming down
through the bell tower and landing on benches of a city
park where no one is sleeping. Covered in snow
they look like polar bears at the zoo. Too knocked up
on heart medication to do anything but lie around and eat.

Dickman's voice has the affable authority and nervy sweetness of Kenneth Koch (from his "Art of Love" period), and it may sound superficially like the absurdist effervescence of other young (and not so young) poets of our moment. But Dickman's poems, I would hurry to say, are not enlisted in the army of irony; clever indeed, they are not "wickedly" clever; they are not trying to credential their own postmodernism, or to prove the acumen of their dislocated linguistics. Rather, they are telling the thousand stories which Whitman called "the myriad peacock speculation of the world."

I feel it is worth emphasizing the narrative dirt underlying this collection, the principle that human life is made of skating rinks and Civil War reenactments, plane crashes and coffee filters happening to persons named Sally and Javier. Stories augmented with lamenting, bragging, fantasy and exhortation. And, as the speaker says in the poem "V," "maybe this is not a giant leap/ into the science of compassion, but it's something."

Not that the news is all sweet in the All-American poem. Plenty of dark corners and sooty intimations lurk inside these genial plentitudes. The poem "Trouble" is a two-page, darkly comic catalogue of public and private figures who committed suicide—

Marilyn Monroe took all her sleeping pills
to bed when she was thirty-six and Marlon Brando's daughter

hung in the Tahitian living room
of her mother's house
while Stanley Adams shot himself in the head.

Yet at the end of this abecedarium of corpses, Dickman's poem arrives at a typically unpretentious yet no less serious rebuttal:

In the morning I get out of bed, I brush
my teeth, I wash my face, I get dressed in the clothes I like best.
I want to be good to myself.

What a good idea. *All-American Poem* is a heroic and generous collection of poetry, and Dickman has a genius which will be enriching our poetry for a long time.

Tony Hoagland

All-American Poem

Part One

The Mysterious Human Heart

The produce in New York is really just produce, oranges
and cabbage, celery and beets, pomegranates
with their hundred seeds, carrots and honey,
walnuts and thirteen varieties of apples.
On Monday morning I will walk down
to the market with my heart inside me, mysterious,
something I will never get to hold
in my hands, something I will never understand.
Not like the apricots and potatoes, the albino
asparagus wrapped in damp paper towels, their tips
like the spark of a match, the bunches of daisies, almost more
a weed than a flower, the clementine,
the sausage links and chicken hung
in the window, facing the street where my heart is president
of the Association for Random Desire, a series
of complex yeas and nays,
where I pick up the plantain, the ginger root, the sprig
of cilantro that makes me human, makes me
a citizen with the right to vote, to bear arms, the right
to assemble and fall in love.

Slow Dance

More than putting another man on the moon,
more than a New Year's resolution of yogurt and yoga,
we need the opportunity to dance
with really exquisite strangers. A slow dance
between the couch and dining room table, at the end
of the party, while the person we love has gone
to bring the car around
because it's begun to rain and would break their heart
if any part of us got wet. A slow dance
to bring the evening home. Two people
rocking back and forth like a buoy. Nothing extravagant.
A little music. An empty bottle of whiskey.
It's a little like cheating. Your head resting
on his shoulder, your breath moving up his neck.
Your hands along her spine. Her hips
unfolding like a cotton napkin
and you begin to think about
how all the stars in the sky are dead. The my body
is talking to your body slow dance. The *Unchained Melody*,
Stairway to Heaven, power-chord slow dance. All my life
I've made mistakes. Small
and cruel. I made my plans.
I never arrived. I ate my food. I drank my wine.
The slow dance doesn't care. It's all kindness like children
before they turn three. Like being held in the arms
of my brother. The slow dance of siblings.
Two men in the middle of the room. When I dance with him,
one of my great loves, he is absolutely human,

and when he turns to dip me
or I step on his foot because we are both leading,
I know that one of us will die first and the other will suffer.
The slow dance of what's to come
and the slow dance of insomnia
pouring across the floor like bath water.
When the woman I'm sleeping with
stands naked in the bathroom,
brushing her teeth, the slow dance of ritual is being spit
into the sink. There is no one to save us
because there is no need to be saved.
I've hurt you. I've loved you. I've mowed
the front yard. When the stranger wearing a sheer white dress
covered in a million beads
slinks toward me like an over-sexed chandelier suddenly come to life,
I take her hand in mine. I spin her out
and bring her in. This is the almond grove
in the dark slow dance.
It is what we should be doing right now. Scraping
for joy. The haiku and honey. The orange and orangutan slow dance.

Some Days

It's winter in Oregon
and I'm thinking about the snow in Ann Arbor
where my brother lives in his happiness,
the masculine huskiness
of corned beef stewing inside its own juices,
filling the heavy-bottomed pot,
big enough to hide a small teenager,
the grease of a thousand mornings
darkening the iron and copper,
the two brown eggs lying on the cutting table, femininity
doubled up, a stereotype in stereo,
the sun breaking over the ladles and knives like water.
Any cook would want to hold them,
their perfectly formed shells,
the yolk inside its yellow limbo, both
in one hand, my brother cracks them over the steel bowl
while the snow falls
like really expensive French sea salt,
the kind that comes in little blue bowls
with cork tops and the words
Sel de Mer written in French loops and flourishes,
like someone's number on a pack of matches
after you've closed a bar or maybe
not even that, not even closed it
but drank real fast so everything
was French and flourishy.
In the morning you can take your hangover to work,
when everything feels more German than French, and work

will straighten you out. Work will make you
see clearly even if, like my friend Mike,
you wake up early so you can deliver candy bars
and soda-pop to the machines
scattered across the University campus
where you used to go to school before taking this job,
putting on the gray jumpsuit, starting up
the truck, the robins staring at you from the barbed wire
fence. He is working
so students can drop their parents' coins
into little slots so that THUNK!
a piece of chocolate or can of cold
Coca-Cola will fall into a larger slot.
Slot to slot Mike worked all day and drank
on the Sabbath with a book or two in his head
and some car in his heart.
When I worked the job opening a café
at five in the morning, I knew beautiful women
were getting out of the shower, drying off, not even thinking
of coffee yet, or the croissants I was making,
folding and re-folding the dough
over the cold marble slab, some hopefulness
pouring out of me, waiting
for them to arrive, the bell
around the doorknob jingling
a little behind them, the bell
somehow like a dimple
above the ass
of a person you love, I can't explain it,
it's somehow silver
and supernatural. It didn't matter.
I never saw them. I worked

in the back, behind the closet
filled with detergents and toilet paper,
until the soups were done and the chicken cleaned,
the guts tossed, the boning knife
washed and sheaved, my apron
covered in blood
darker than the darkest cigar.
Some days a kitchen can
save your life. Carl would
come in and have one piece of brown
pumpkin bread, reading the *Times* or the *Oregonian*
or that late, great magazine, *The Sciences*,
where even a guy from Harvard, Illinois could understand
biophysics. Every time he opened
The New Yorker, each time he picked up
the warm bread
and placed it to his red mouth, he was not
thinking of how much he'd lost
or who he would love desperately
with nothing but wind
moving through his hands like a rope.
When I was broke and hungry and worried about the dogwood trees
I thought of my brother
making croutons and blintzes in Michigan,
the corned beef steaming,
the sun with its yolk running over everything.
I thought of him, and almost,
as if he had pulled it from his own wallet,
a ten dollar bill lay folded
on the sidewalk where I picked it up
and went directly out to lunch, a bowl of onion soup, a pint of dark
beer, the bread was free, and all because

of my brother, that old apron,
that great and mythic friend of mine,
that lucky charm.

At Night My Hat

At night my hat disappears.
And then my coat, scarf, gloves, my watch with the time inside it
bravely marching forward. I wish I had a dog to walk.
I wish I had an animal to feed and clean up after. Something
to make a noise when I get home, to see the shadow
of my hat and wag its tail in acceptance.
The hat resting softly with its complex history of masculine principles:
helmets and berets, stocking caps, Stetsons. Ten-gallon
Texans and Australian straws.
Did my grandfather wear one the nights he took my grandmother
to the white speakeasies outside Chinatown?
And my brother? What is he wearing while the snow in Detroit
falls on all the new cars? My father once wore a lampshade.
Life of the party circa 1975.
I wore a cowboy hat until my head grew, then I replaced it with a red plastic
fireman's engine #9. Made new plans. Had new dreams.
The hat which disappeared tonight was a good hat. Something
I could have worn in the garden, something
I could have worn downtown. Mon chapeau! The hat I love
has gone back to Panama and Germany, Texas and bitter South Dakota.

Classical Poem

I'm listening to a symphony where Heroes and Villains are still alive.
Not a soundtrack of soldiers parachuting into occupied Belgium
but spies in pinstripes. Not a dark forest
lit up by gunfire and the wild eyes of a lost elk
but a dark alley, a cobblestone alley, an alley where important
documents are being passed between the black leather gloves
of important men
near a window where a barmaid is pouring lager into dim glasses.
It's the kind of music to make love to
with a shy woman who works all day at the public library,
her breasts roaring like the two lions outside.
It's what I imagine astronauts are listening to
inside their helmets
while they watch a new planet begin to spin,
and then another and another like notes from a cello until the night sky
looks like an aquarium,
full of the mystical and unreal. Space dust
floating through a dark channel, a movable space
relaxing into itself. I'll tell you
the composer's name is Valentin Silvestrov
and I know as much about him as the umbrella I bought yesterday
knows about me. The radio program
says that this is the music of existential metaphor, silent songs,
which I do understand. I have them all the time.
When I first saw your feet, for instance. The curve and bright white
of them. The time you walked into my room
wearing your father's El Dorado hat and said
I am not my father. This is not his hat. Well, I thought,

you must be suffering
and that it was life, the crestfallen drive-thru,
that was making you cry. But it was me.
And I'm no one in particular. I'm certainly not
Valentin Silvestrov living in 80's Berlin, all the West like a giant carrot
dangling in the blue sky and Rilke's angels
haunting him, following him
into the bathroom at night, waiting for him on the street
after someone the composer knew had died and it had, for this to be classical,
begun to snow. Heroes and Villains killing each other in half
and quarter notes. Valentin putting on his great coat
with a rip in the lapel. Walking out toward the traffic. Walking home
and eventually lying down, like all of us, in the well-made, unbearable bed.

Love

We fall in love at weddings and auctions, over glasses
of wine in Italian restaurants
where plastic grapes hang on the lattice, our bodies throb
in the checkout line, bookstores, the bus stop,
and we can't keep our hands off each other
until we can—
so we turn to rubber masks and handcuffs, falling in love again.
We go to movies and sit in the air-conditioned dark
with strangers who are in love
with heroes like Peter Parker
who loves a girl he can't have
because he loves saving the world in red and blue tights
more than he would love to have her ankles wrapped around
his waist or his tongue between her legs.
While we watch films
in which famous people play famous people
who experience pain,
the boy who sold us popcorn loves the girl
who sold us our tickets
and stares at the runs in her stockings each night,
even though she is in love
with the skinny kid who sells her cigarettes at the 7-11
and if the world had any compassion
it would let the two of them pass a Marlboro Light
back and forth
until their fingers eventually touched, their mouths sucking
and blowing. If the world knew how
much they loved each other

then we would all be better off. We could all dive head first
into the sticky parts. We could make sweat
a religion. We could light a candle
and praise the holiness of smelliness. Imagine standing
beneath the gothic archways of feet,
the gilded bowls of armpits. Who doesn't want to kneel down
and pray before the altar of the mouth?
For my part I am going to stop
right here,
on this dark night,
on this country road,
where country songs come from, and kiss her, this woman,
below the trees,
which are below the stars,
which are below desire.
There's a music to it. I can hear it.
Johnny Cash, Biggie Smalls, Johann Sebastian Bach, I don't care
what they say. I loved you
the way my mouth loves teeth,
the way a boy I know would risk it all for a purple dinosaur,
who, truth be told, loved him.
There is no accounting for it.
In fact there are no accountants
balancing the books of love, measuring
the heart's distance and speed.
In the Midwest, for instance,
there are fields of corn madly in love with a scarecrow,
his potato-sack head
and straw body, standing among the dog-eared stalks,
his arms stretched out like a farm-Christ
full of love. Turning on the radio
I know how much AM loves FM. It's the same way

my mother loved Elvis
whose hips all young girls love, sitting around the television
in poodle skirts and bobby socks,
watching him move across the screen like something
even sex dreamed of having.
He loved me tender for so many years
that I was born after a long night of Black Russians and Canasta
while *Jailhouse Rock* rocked.
I love the way my screen door, if it isn't latched shut,
will fling itself open to the wind,
how the clouds above me look like animals covered in milk.
And I'm not the only one.
Stamps love envelopes. The licking proves it.
Just look at my dog
who obviously loves himself with an intensity
no human being could sustain, though you can't say we don't try.
The S&M goddess
who brings her husband to the mall,
dressed in a leather jumper, leading him through the food court
by a leash. The baker who scores
his wife's name into the thin skin of the pumpernickel
before peeling it into the oven.
Once a baby lizard loved me so completely
he moved into my apartment and died of hunger.
I was living there with a girl who loved to say the word
shuttlecock. She would call
me at work and whisper shuttlecock
into my ear which loved it! The blastoff
of the first word sending the penis into space.
Not that I ever imagined
my cock being a spaceship,
though sometimes men are like astronauts, orbiting

the hot planets of women,
amazed that they have traveled so far, wanting
to land, wanting to document the first walk,
the first moan,
but never truly understanding what
has moved them. Love in an elevator.
Love in the backseat of your parent's Chevette.
Love going to college, cutting her hair, reading Plath and sleeping
with other girls.
Sometimes love is lying across the bed
but it might not be yours.
And sometimes it travels into a hostile territory
where it's hardly recognizable
but there all the same.
I know a man who loves tanks so much
he wishes he had one
to pick up the groceries, drive
his wife to work, drop his daughter off
at school with her Little Mermaid
lunch box, a note
hidden inside, next to the apple, folded
with a love that can be translated into any language: I hope
you do not suffer.

The Black Album

Black like my sister's black eye an imaginary father
gave her, so now she is forever beaten
by the absence of men, her pupil,
black like a record is black.
Black like my coffee mug but not my coffee
for I drink it with cream. For I walk out
onto the beach and bless the black bottoms
of the boats, for the plankton glow
inside the black sea like white blood cells.
For music and poverty are the great regulators of the world
when white kids in Kansas are bumping Tupac
from the windows of Ford pickups, working
in the canneries, dreaming of LA: raving and mad
between the turntables. The more I listen to Jay-Z
the more I'm reminded of Led Zeppelin,
The Stones, how they begin to live
the same life. How they need each other like organs
from a greater body. And then there are the black
keys Mr. Mozart bent into sound
so the people in the castle would have something
to move them, when outside the sky was black
and so was the moor, someone walking
across it, lost in his own suffering,
but a part of everything, the bog, the moon, the man
on the moon with his black dinner jacket, his teeth
bright black and earth below with its factories
pumping like a dog's heart pumps after its owner
drives up, opens the door, calls out its name.

Black like the buttons on your grandfather's coat
and black like the suits we wear
when our grandfathers die. I'm telling you
it's hard to tell the rivers apart from the hills, the super-malls
from the ma and pa's when I feel them both
so acutely. Black like licorice used to be
and black like the lace bra Susan wore
beneath a baby-blue t-shirt
and how I would take her to the mat like a wrestler
and how she would keep her black boots on
so that now when I think of black boots I am no longer thinking
of Neo Nazis or soldiers but bedrooms and bedposts.
She had a black pair of handcuffs with black feathers
so that it looked like a black bird of submission.
For she was good when bound up
by black leather belts, for what we did
we did in the black voice box of evening
and in the morning the light came in
to touch her where she slept, drooling on the pillow.
David wrote "I don't know,
now, if any of us get out of this."
And I'm not sure any of us would want to,
the world coming together, crashing
around us, while we drive through the forests of Vermont,
listening to *The Black Album,* blasting it,
and the black bear that leaps from the road onto the tree
like a heavy black star, so that later
I would think of blackberries growing off
the freeway, the way you feel when you're moving
along like a train running, furious, on all this black coal.

Public Parks

This one is named after a suffragist and it's also the first place,
at night near a pond where families of ducks
float by like paper boats, I felt
the warm legs of covered-in-shadow romance and had no idea what
to do with my hands.
I remember how her tights were smooth
but scratchy and midnight blue, she had
dark curly hair and a name like Ramon. Or maybe
it was Simone and her tongue was perfect like her knees
and the weeping willow wept hard for us
because we were rough and rough with each other as much as we were kind.
There was a bridge over part of the pond
and I crossed it when it rained and Simone
wore a shirt that looked like water
when you looked into it and saw a sky that was not
a sky and your face which was not really a face. The park was open
all night with patrol cars moving in and out, their bodies
like heavy benevolent animals.
There we were with our clothes half-torn and soaked. This is my favorite
memory of rain and parks and ducks and nylon stockings.
I like parks with statues
and parks with fountains.
I have sat below a few signatories
of several important American papers while pigeons
sat above them, on their shoulders, swords, and wrists.
Lincoln stands, among other places, in the park near a famous bookstore
where he is turning green, facing Alder Street
and Rich's Cigar Shop where you can get a really nice Romeo y Juliette

and smoke it on a park bench near the YMCA.
Some parks are celebrated for the bushes that men hide behind,
touching each other in the dangerous hour
before returning home
to their wives and boyfriends, setting a table and pulling a roast from the oven.
Some parks are noted for their baseball fields and some for their swing sets.
Some for their willows
and some for a body that's found by hikers, left in the wet
brown leaves for the worms and twelve o'clock news,
the reporter combing his hair
between takes. I have performed Shakespeare
in the parks. I played a wall and fell in love
with a girl who played a nymph,
she wore a green dress made out of vinyl leaves that shimmered and shook
above her hips. She had a lazy eye and listened to Patti Smith.
There's a park I visit whenever I'm in Chicago
and one in NYC where I smoke German cigarettes and watch students pass
between classes, all the lamps covered
by decorative, giant lampshades. The students
with their Norton anthologies
writing papers about George Herbert and Henry James,
some in love with professors and some
with little burns on their ankles
because a lover tied them too tight between the bed posts
and some with no one at all and no bed at all
but a blow-up mattress they pump full of air
each night before reading a section of the *Iliad,*
fighting themselves to sleep.
I like the secret life of students almost as much as I like parks
like the one in Texas where garbage cans are hidden behind a mosaic
of multi-colored tile so you're not even thinking of garbage
but Adobe Flats, Mesas, and in particular a collage by Ray Johnson

and a tabletop by my neighbor who also cuts words
out of the daily crossword puzzle
and pastes them onto a separate page, making poems
that are often sad and terrifying. Can you believe it,
he says, these words were just lying there in twenty-four down and eight across.
He and I used to walk to a park that was five feet
by six feet, one live oak to sit beneath and one large stone to set a book
or a baby on. You could eat lunch there if it was a small lunch
and you were alone.
I dropped acid and walked through a park where I met myself over and over
until I was afraid that I wasn't anyone at all.
I drank Australian beer with Carl in a park known for its roses, high
above the city, and we talked about his brother who was dying
of cancer and the girl he was seeing
who wiped his brow and left him at the same time.
Carl read a poem about Prospero that Jack Gilbert wrote when Jack Gilbert
was living in Greece. This park is surrounded
by barbed wire like a nasty halo, filled with kids in rainboots
who know the pleasures of mud and kings.
I knelt down in this park, below
a redwood tree and pretended
I was Saint Francis of Assisi though the birds were afraid of me.
I like this park because it's like a small car
clowns pile out of, one after the other, and you think there's a trap door
underneath, but there isn't. This park
is where everyone goes on the fourth
of July to eat watermelon and watch the sky explode.
This park is the smallest park in the world, named after the poet
Hazel Hall who no one reads anymore and maybe never did.
This park is so big it should be National but it isn't, its Public like the library
and all of us can go there with frisbees and water bottles.
You could be standing inside it

near the sandbox, your shirt unbuttoned at the top, a little
sand brushed away from your neck, some small
sparkling grains of which have fallen
beneath the wire and fabric of your push-up bra and later after we've taken
our walk and had our picnic, after the dog is tired
of catching the ball and we drive home, the sand turning into salt, the park closing
behind us, I am going to take you into the bedroom
and lick it off.

An Imaginary French Film

What a delight. Walking arm in arm
toward the artsy movie theater
that shows movies when they're American and films when they're French.
All those dark streets of Paris!
All those Parisians looking up at the moon, looking back
into each others eyes, looking up at the moon
and getting all turned around because what else is la vie but to look
at the moon once in a while and then
smash! right on the kisser. Ah Love. Ah Paris when it's raining
and dark and I'm having popcorn in the dark,
watching the march of subtitles make their way across the shoulders
and breasts of actors from Lyon and actresses from Marseilles,
raised on farms but beautiful and moody like Warren Beatty was
when he turned eighteen and looked at the moon and cried.
He looked up with tears running down his cheeks
and cried *mon dieu*! Which means Jesus Christ! when you're living
on the West Coast and your great-grandfather knew people
who killed Indians so the world would be safe enough
to grow up poor with a single mother
who was a hero and a hammer. We can sit quietly
until the credits rise up like dust behind a horse and carriage.
I will look out across the sea of red velvet theater-seats,
all connected like a royal archipelago,
and your hair will be tied back like a dark cloud
or let down around your shoulders like its own kind of sea,
before walking home along a road that was very near, in fact,
very near the sea.

Snow

1

Let's put on our gloves and scarves
and walk out under the birches
into the white world!
We can make snow angels with Rockefeller and most
of Harvard Law. The white world I'm talking about.
The Kennedy brothers and snowball fights when all the roads leaving
Hyannis are covered in black ice
and wouldn't my grandmother be happy if her dead president
was alive and well and drinking hot chocolate.
The milkish crunch beneath our boots
and the bright blue breath rising from our mouths like smokestacks.
Each of us his own train puffing up the cold hill
where Teddy lets go one giant frozen pumpkin that gathers like age
layer after layer of snow on its descent into the street below
where cars are frozen shut and cannot be driven or else
they slip and slide
and can kill somebody. Santa is somewhere in red leather
smoking a pipe that smells like cinnamon.
He is Christmas-white the same way Jesus is, sleeping
in a cradle somewhere in Palo Alto,
below the twinkling lights of a Starbucks
where candy cane mochas
are flying out the window like geese
out of hell. It is fucking co-old
out here. The big flakes coming down
through the bell tower and landing on the benches of a city

park where no one is sleeping. Covered in snow
they look like polar bears at the zoo. Too knocked up
on heart medication to do anything else but lie around and eat. The park
is quiet like blankets are quiet
and I put my hand into Jackie's back pocket to get a lighter
for my cigarette but also for obvious reasons.
How her snow pants fit
around her ass and how I didn't want to be alone that night but was.

2

I wrote your name in the snow but only got to the second R
before I had to go back in and drink another beer. I was so close
and in the blue light the yard was making
with the moon your name looked like something
carved by an ice skate worn by a gold medalist
famous for his flirting
and connected in some circles to the Norwegian judge.

I give you an eight
for putting up with me. I give you a ten for sleeping in the igloo
I built out of everything that had fallen that day.

3

I can't tell you how strangely romantic the Atlantic becomes when the sky
is dumping snow into it. It's like seeing, for the first time,
a naked body. Even though you know her name. You have even played a part
in making her naked, but now she is something
altogether different. Something altogether secret, like under-the-bed-secrets
when you were five and there were really monsters in the world.
Snow and sand. You can make a snowman

with a lobster claw pipe, a pebble nose, and two eyes made out of shells.
White shells some creature used to live inside of.
Pebbles ground down from the great rocks
they used to be. A claw pulled apart by seagulls, the body still hard
and match-box red. I make one next to a row of overturned rowboats
covered in ice and white like the top of Mt. Hood
even in summer. That's the magic of mountains
besides the mist and the fact that some of them will blow up, a blizzard of ash
covering hundreds of miles.
I wrap a scarf around my snowman and give him a name
so we can be formally introduced. I light a small cigar
and give it to him but he lets it die.
We talk about how high the winds are
until the hat I gave him flies off and goes tumbling
down the snow covered beach, me running after it
because my sister made it for me
and there is something about winter and sibling rivalry I can't live without.

Part Two

Byron Loves Me

My dead English professor sits at the foot
of my bed, crying.
What's the matter? I ask.
Matthew, he says, I will never understand Byron.
My wife is married to another man, my daughter is in love
with pop songs about sex
and money, while Byron offers nothing
but Seville and oranges. I can't tell if he loves
me or not. My professor shrugs
like all dead men
shrug, stands up and walks out
of my room like all men, dead or alive, slowly
with his head bent to the task of leaving. Waking up
in the early morning, half dressed
for a dream about ballroom dancing—my coattails fluttering
in long black strips behind me, top hat
pulled down over my eyes
and half-dressed for breakfast—my pajama bottoms
covered with flickering hotel signs,
I remember that I live alone.
And because I live alone
I take the palm trees far too seriously, depend
far too much on my books
lined up like a third grade class preparing for recess,
all wearing different coats, some
pushing and pulling at their classmates. If you live
alone with a smile
thin as a paper cut, your dead English professor coming

around every other night in tears,
an empty mailbox and a neighbor
that puts her cigarettes out in your begonia
You should not hang yourself.
Tell the palm tree you love him. Light a candle
and offer yourself up to the books.
Haven't they saved your life once before? Reading
Allen Ginsberg the day your friend cut himself open
in the backseat of his car,
the engine running while his mother
was getting high off a plastic bag
of paint thinner, a bluish ring around her mouth.
You could have been in that car. You could have
been like her
but you sat on the floor and pulled Lucille Clifton
off the shelf instead.
As if that were not enough
to make you shiver
while the angel of fate passed you over, somewhere
in New Jersey
you have Bruce Springsteen
writing songs about you and wondering how you are.

V

The skinny girl walking arm-in-arm
with her little sister
is wearing a shirt that says
TALK NERDY TO ME
and I want to,
I want to put my bag of groceries down
beside the fire hydrant
and whisper something in her ear
about long division.
I want to stand behind her and run
a single finger down her spine
while she tells me about all her correlatives.
Maybe she'll moan a little
when I tell her that x equals negative-b
plus or minus the square root
of b-squared minus 4(a)(c) all over
2a. I have my hopes.
I could show her my comic books
and Play Station. We could pull out
my old D&D cards
and sit in the basement with a candle lit.
I know enough about Dr.Who
and the Star Fleet Enterprise
to get her shirt off, to unbutton her jeans.
We could work out String Theory
all over her bedroom.
We could bend space together.
But maybe that's not what she's asking.

The world 's been talking dirty
ever since she's had the ears to listen.
It's been talking sleazy to all of us
and there's nothing about the hydrogen bomb
that makes me want to wear a cock ring
or do it in the kitchen while a pot of water boils.
Maybe, with her shoulders slouched
the way they are and her long hair
covering so much of her face,
she's asking, simply, to be considered
something more than a wild night, a tight
curl of pubic hair, the pink,
complicated, structures of nipples.
Maybe she wants to be measured beyond
the teaspoon shadow of the anus
and the sweet mollusk of the tongue,
beyond the equation of limbs and seen
as a complete absolute.
And maybe this is not a giant leap
into the science of compassion, but it's something.
So when I pass her
I do exactly what she has asked of me,
I raise my right hand and make a V
the way Vulcans do when they wish someone well,
hoping she gets what she wants, even
if it has to be in a galaxy far away.

Roma

Last night my neighbor was looking a little enlightened,
you know, the way bodies do
after spending the afternoon having sex
on an old couch while responsible people are suffering
with their clothes on in cubicles and libraries.
He had that look vegetables get
in really nice grocery stores where the tomatoes aren't just red
they're goddamn red!
He was like that. Like a glowing, off-the-vine Roma
sitting in his living room picking pineapple off a Hawaiian pizza
and telling me about his father who was a real mother
fucker. I ask him if he still loved his dad, or if he loved him more
now that he is dead. *Sure*, he says, *I love anything that's dead.*
Someone's hand floats up onto the beach
while the body is still lost below the current, a vase of lilacs
turned brown, the black archipelago of mourners marching
up the hill. My neighbor is there to greet each of them
with a box of chocolates and a barbershop quartet in the background.
When my father died, he says opening a beer, *he was no longer*
my father. He was no longer a man. It's easy to love things
when they're powerless, like children and goldfish.
This is the way with enlightened people. They say things
that are so infuriatingly simple when the world is not.
So I put down my Pepsi and pull out the big card.
What about Hitler? I ask. *You can't love Hitler!*
My neighbor puts a piece of pineapple on his tongue like a sacrament,
sucks the juice out of it, chews it up, then turns
his head slow like a cloud and says *I can love anybody I feel like loving.*

And I say *that's ridiculous.*
And he says *what's ridiculous is that you don't.* And there he is again,
shining in the grocery store, pulling the bow off
the heart-shaped candies and putting one softly into his father's mouth.

Thanksgiving Poem

A few days after the smoke cleared in the South
and the muskets were hung
in the dining rooms of the North,
President Lincoln announced a National Day
of Thanksgiving. So that every god-fearing citizen
of these United States could sit down, leave the past
for the dead, and have dinner.
To think of a simpler time full of beads, corn, peace-pipes,
and the magical largesse of Plymouth Rock:
Them Indians and them Pilgrims and them Indians, what a meal!
All's forgiven, every year, and that goes for my house too.
Even if we don't cook at home
but lose ourselves in the Teutonic
gastronomy of The Berlin House,
which is really pronounced Das Berliner Hausen,
with its fraulein waitresses
and pasta the Germans call schnitzel.
I had turkey. Turkey and cabbage and schnitzel
and a glass of dark beer. It was loud in there
and the poor Germans with all their poor politics behind them
were working overtime. Well, from one culture
that almost wiped out another
to another culture who almost wiped out
one of the oldest in the world, I'd like to say, fucking-hell
was it weird having dinner with you!
Weird but somehow exactly as I always
imagined Thanksgiving to be. Something beyond yams.
And it was. My ninety-three-year-old grandmother

ate almost four desserts. My mother looked about to cry.
My sister looked like she was going to ignite. The family
sitting next to us were talking loudly
about the Mormons, whom they thought
were a cult that worshiped space aliens.
But they were Catholics and believed in eating flesh,
drinking blood, and a magical zombie
who walks out of a cave after being dead for three days.
The woman taking their order looked like a pixie
or a pagan with a long tattoo crawling out of her
black skirt. The tattoo looked like an alphabet.
Some sentence she couldn't live without,
some line from a song, and now she can't see it but for a mirror
or a lover back there softly reading it aloud. Oh Germany!
I think you might have made clocks once. And that was nice.
For our part, we set a table
with the nice old Indians and ate corn
on the cob, mashed potatoes, stuffing,
eventually naming professional football teams after them
so we could go on fighting forever.
But I should be giving thanks
instead of harping on about all the bad things in the world.
So here's some thanks for hula-hoops
and baseball cards and the time in the fourth grade
when one of the Schmidt twins
kissed me behind an oak tree,
and thanks to *The Indian in the Cupboard*
which I read that year and still think about
every September, thanks to the lunch-line
ladies that gave me extra Tater Tots
and thanks to after-school programs
like the one my siblings and I attended

where we learned to Jazzercise
and stretch our little muscles. I want to thank
watermelon in the summer
and Hitchcock movies in the winter,
especially his film *Rebecca*
because now my brother and I say
you can never go back
to Mandalay but really we mean
I miss you, you live so far away. Thanks
to coffee beans and coffee, the warm
smell of steamed milk and people putting
cappuccinos to their mouths
so that there is a moment
like lovemaking when their mouths are covered in cream.
Thanks for doorknobs and Post-it notes,
for tire-swings and corn-dogs,
for all the socks I have ever worn
and for all the people that I've chosen to be mean to,
those who endured my small unfeeling actions
with such grace, and thanks as well to Grace and God
and the Holy Ghost of Shopping Malls
where everything seems golden and sweet.
Thanks and the giving of Thanks. Dinner
at the Berlin House was wonderful
even after we figured out how much
everybody owed and what the tip should be,
when we put on our coats and said Guden Nacht
to the Hessians, Labanact to the Lithuanians,
and Aila Tov to the Jews,
a glass doll sitting on the window ledge
opened her terrible eyes and then closed them again.

Amigos

When money will have nothing to do with me,
when the only voice I hear is my own
and all my books are having a great laugh at my expense—
especially Lowell
who doesn't think I'm a man at all—
I go to the café and sit among my amigos.
The woman whose left arm has blossomed into skulls and roses is my sister.
The man in the business suit, wrapped like a muzzle around his body,
is talking on the phone with a client. The client is my brother.
The man is my confidant.
At any moment California will fall into the Pacific
and this congregation of ours will rise up
and walk across the Barnes & Noble parking lot
toward those great breaking waves.
We will be together
in car accidents, train wrecks,
in a hot bath clouding up with our own blood
while the men and women we love read quietly in the other room,
in emergency landings,
with twelve-year-olds carrying their fathers' pistols to class,
we will look and see each other.
There are days I feel as though someone has written my name on a stone
and thrown it over the side of a cliff.
Sometimes I pour milk into my coffee
and I look at the paper and know
what has pulled me from bed;
it has hidden in every part of my body,
waited for me in hotels like a pillow mint,

filled my ears with music,

rubbed against me at parties,

it's been an infant and it's been an e-mail.

We bomb a mosque. They mutilate a body.

When a man from Indiana keeps the fingernails of the waitresses he kills,

and on the facing page balloons float softly around the words

g r a n d o p e n i n g,

I feel like a dog that is sniffing the ass of another dog,

who in turn wishes that she was tied back up in the yard.

I want to be with everyone here,

with their lattes and mochas,

while the water rises

and the top of the Golden Gate bridge is blinking in the surf,

when the aliens land and eat us,

as soldiers from another country drag us by the hair

from our yards,

while the valley is flooded and all its talk about vastness and god has drowned,

I want to know their names, mis amigos,

their hands reaching out toward mine,

when the flights are rerouted

away from our loved ones, let's all lift a glass or child into the air,

open-mouthed

as we watch the final cruelty performed simultaneously

with the last kindness.

All-American Poem

I want to peel off a hundred dollar bill
and slap it down on the counter.
You can pick out a dress. I'll pick out a tie: polka dots
spinning like disco balls. Darling let's go
two-stepping in the sawdust at the Broken Spoke.
Let's live downtown and go clubbing.
God save hip-hop and famous mixed drinks.
Let's live in a cardboard box. Let's live
in a loft above Chelsea, barely human, talking about
the newest collection of Elizabeth Peyton,
her brilliant strokes, the wine and cheese.
You can go from one state to another and never
paint the same thing twice. In New Mexico
we could live by a creek and hang our laundry
on the line. Let's get naked in the cold waters of Michigan.
Let's get hitched in Nevada. Just you, me, and Elvis.
We could sell cheese curd in Wisconsin.
We could rent the sky in Montana.
I could pay off my bills. You could strip
in some dive on the outskirts of Pittsburgh.
Let's bite each other on the neck.
Oh my sexy Transylvania!
We could be relationship counselors
for trannies in South Dakota.
It must be hard to have a woman living
inside you
when you're watching cows chew
the frozen grass of December.

You are everywhere, sweet Carolinas.
You're my boss, Tennessee, you honeysuckle.
Give us a kiss Hawaii. Who says we're not an Empire? Fuck 'em,
they need Jesus. They need the Holy Ghost.
Right Kansas? Kansas! My yellow brick road of intelligent design. We are not
monkeys. They're all in prison, right Texas? Texas,
I was with you on the fourth of July watching the sky undress
with my friends
and we were Americans on America Day,
which is every day,
coming home from work, drinking a beer
and waiting for the dark,
for the night, the rocket's red glare, lying around
on a blanket in the backyard, a girl from your hometown
leaning against you, slipping
her slender foot in and out of a saltwater sandal. She's wearing
cherry lip balm and taking ecstacy.
Later you can taste it.
The smooth wax along her mouth, her arms
stretched out in the grass and each narrow leaf of grass
like a separate lover, the horizon
of a summer tan rising above her low-cut jeans.
She looks different here than she did in her uniform, standing behind
the counter of the Coffee-Go, steaming milk,
rows of flavored syrup above her head: almond, blackberry, mint, vanilla.
This is the Fourth of July
and she looks like the end of summer. She's a wind
moving through the trees. She's the best thing
about high school assemblies. We are a country at war
and she's passing a note to you in class, your book open
to the chapter on dissecting frogs. How to keep the brain intact
when removing it from the small skull. The note says

why were you holding Clare's hand after lunch?
We are a country at war but it's not really happening
here. It is not Clare or her brother or all the bourbon
in Kentucky. On the Fourth of July
I walk out among the fallen
watermelon rinds, the corn cobs, paper plates with chicken grease
being pushed by a little breeze
so they look like moons spun out of orbit.
I go inside. I turn the television on.
It's playing the Civil War again. The Battle of Gettysburg
remembering itself on the football field
at Lincoln Memorial High. A rush of gray uniforms
poised on the scrimmage line. The poor sons of Alabama
wearing the uniforms of dead soldiers.
The North marching down
toward cotton revenue and Big Tobacco. The South starving,
fighting, often without shoes, the narrator explaining
how the muskets were loaded, fired, and then re-loaded.
That's a lot of time
to think about the person you're killing.
That's a lot of time to wish you were home.
Unless, of course, you were home
and your house was burning down. Out of the smoke
there's always more smoke. There's always the hacking apart and crying.
You can go from one Civil War to another
and still not be free. The man in charge of the antique cannon
has lit his shirt on fire. The man in charge
of the horse runs Ray's Hardware on 10th and Main.
He's having a liquidation sale this weekend.
The show is over
in an hour. That includes commercials
and the slow, I won't kill you, pace

of the re-enactment. This is how it happened,
the narrator is saying,
while his producer plays a negro spiritual. It makes you weep.
The vocalist calling out to God. Oh Lord! Oh Lord my God, she's singing,
have pity on our souls. You can go from one state
to another and pity will meet you at the Grayhound Station.
In the stands of the Lincoln Memorial football field
a little boy is eating cotton candy while the dead men rise up
from the twenty-yard line and walk toward their families. I love
the History Channel. It's so foreign. The old reels of Germany
having the fascism bombed out of it. Kennedy waving
from the black sedan. It's almost real. Boston grieving. Pulling its hair out.
You can take the Chinatown bus from Boston
to the Chinatown in New York City. You can go
from one shop window
with peeled ducks hanging by their ankles
to another shop window
with peeled ducks hanging by their ankles.
In Oregon you can go from one hundred-year-old evergreen
to another hundred-year-old evergreen and never turn around.
They're everywhere, cut down
and loaded up, like paperbacks in bookstores.
My favorite bookstore is in Evanston, Illinois.
The owner is Polish and his daughter wore a wool skirt
that kept sliding up her legs
as she sat on the edge of his desk. God bless her
for it was cold outside and I was almost alone
but for my copy of *The Idiot* I carried with me everywhere.
You can go from one Russian novel
to another Russian novel and never have
borsht. You can go from one daughter to another
and eventually end up with your own. You can go from one

Founding Father to another and still have the same
America. The same Alaska. The same Baked Alaska
served on a silver plate in the same hotel
where the wait staff are all South American.
The same cows sleeping
in the same Wyoming with the same kids
getting drunk, shooting cans, peeing on the electric fence.
The same Main Street with the same True Value. The same
flags staggered between the streetlights
like marathon runners. I walked down that street in Tacoma, Washington
with Jennifer when Jennifer had red hair and listened
to Broadway musicals. We smoked
cigarettes in the town square
below a statue of one soldier carrying another. The plaque
read "Brothers in Arms." One soldier carrying another
in his arms. We were young and mean
and thought it was funny. You can go from one town square
to another and never fall in love.
Even in New Hampshire where people *Live Free or Die*.
What kind of life is that
when you're on the road and the woman
next to you is hardly there, hardly speaking, her feet
on the dashboard like two very different promises.
How are you supposed to drive
under these conditions? Forget about the rain. Forget
about Vermont and the Green Mountains' majesty.
Forget Ted Nugent.
Forget Tom Petty and the Heartbreakers.
Forget the swimming pools in California
because if she doesn't love you
what chance have you got with LA?
In LA you don't get to be lonely.

You get skin peels and mud masks.
You can go from one spa to another
and watch the same lemon slices of cucumber
float above the eyes of thirteen-year-old girls and seventy-year-old
women. You won't see that in Minnesota.
Minnesota! cover me up in a wool blanket
and put me to bed. Let me sleep.
Let me have the dream again
where Kenneth Koch walks through my mother's house
looking for a leash. He's taking my dog for a walk. The dog
is scratching at the front door and Kenneth is saying yes, yes, I'm coming.
You can hear him telling the dog that one broken heart
deserves a heart that has been differently broken.
I had that dream in New York City. Times Square
looks like America throwing up on itself.
I want to hold its hair back. I want to sit in the park
where my brother and I drank coffee and ate donuts from Dean & Deluca.
We watched a man fly a little wooden airplane over the green benches.
We ate lunch at the Cedar Tavern.
The french fries I ordered were covered in pepper
like the poem Frank O'Hara wrote to Mayakovsky, saying
I love you. I love you,
but I'm turning to my verses
and my heart is closing
like a fist. The burger was bloody in the middle as if it wasn't through living.
My first girlfriend refused to eat meat.
She said she wouldn't be a tomb for another living creature.
But she privately cut herself on the arms
which confused both her parents.
Senior year she moved to Idaho. I miss her, my sweet potato.
You can go from one state to another
and still hate yourself. Hide in your room listening to The Cure, carving

little commas in your skin. You can go
to Arizona State and never leave your past behind. Arizona waiting
with open arms for the new blood. The great white hope
of tailgate parties and college football. Put me in coach, I'm ready to play!
I'm ready for the lobster rolls of Maine
and the co-eds of Maryland. In Maryland
I played miniature golf with a waitress from Denny's.
I spent the winter sitting in her section, drinking Pepsi,
watching her hips hydroplane inside a green polyester skirt.
It was the year my Uncle Joe died. He was a G.I.
He was a G.I. Joe. A man who hid under the table
if a car backfired. He refused to eat rice.
He came back from Normandy
wanting ice cream. He had a friend from Arkansas
who ended up all over his uniform. An ear burned
into the helmet. He had a friend from Colorado
who got his hands cut off, slow, and forever. His pal
from New Jersey was thrown into the sky
like a human constellation of broken teeth. You can go
from one state to another and still feel pretty good about enlisting.
Joe lived in a trance. Love saved him.
He would scratch his wife's name over and over into the tough leather
of his boots. Hidden below the view-line
of a foxhole, his knife drawn, the word Alice, written like a child
writes on the chalkboard. Alice, Alice,
like an antidote for death. Joe died in a hospital.
You can go from one pool of blood
to another and never see your own reflection.
Oh Mississippi, I worry about your boys.
Oklahoma City, Oklahoma, are you half empty?
Washington D.C., the sons of senators
are sleeping between flannel sheets.

Darling let's go to Florida and sit
in the shade of an orange grove shack.
Let's meet some Cubans and Jews. The world is so big.
Why stay up all night and only have ourselves to keep warm?
I've never been to West Virginia. What the hell
are West Virginians doing this weekend? Or Iowans? In Iowa
there's a new Wal-Mart opening and I'm gonna shed some dimes.
We'll take a bus there. A bus is a diplomat.
It throws us all together, our books,
hats, and umbrellas. I am never more human
than when I'm riding next to someone
who makes me shudder. If my body
touches his body who knows what will happen? Race issues
and cooties. The great unknown
coming home from work. You can go from one state to another
and still not know how to act. We are losing ourselves. We are somewhere
in Delaware. You are my Georgia peach. Your love
is like a field of buffalo when we still had buffalo and they looked like dark
rolling hills deep in North Dakota. America
I'm in love with your imports and exports,
your embargoes and summits!
Let's walk down to the river. Let's bless the paper
boats and turn the whole thing into wine. We can sit quietly on a blanket,
watching the transcendentalists come and go, talking
of Henry David Thoreau. Take me to the river,
Ohio, put me in the water.
Missouri goes down to the river and drinks Vanilla Cokes.
Rhode Island goes down and prays for money.
Connecticut goes down and washes its clothes on the sandy bank.
We go down to the river and the moon
pulls up in its silver Cadillac.
America, let's put our feet in the water! Let's tie a rock

around our waist and jump in.
The moon is revving up. The river
is rolling by. Tom Petty is singing about a girl from Indiana
and I am buying you another drink. I am trying to take you home.

Sad Little Outlaw

Tied to the tree, as I was, while my brother galloped
through the backyard, straddling a broom,
a plastic six-shooter in his hand.
I was always being left behind
in the mud, a bandage around my eyes,
until he reached out
just enough so that our fingers slipped apart
and he could ride away, calling out my name as the posse advanced.
But it wasn't really my name
with its biblical limitations, no, he called out Johnny!!!
Johnny, that all-American from Kansas and Iowa, that Johnny
from New Jersey and Queens, a boy
people will beat their chests for as the flag is being folded
into its triangle of pity.
I was a sad little outlaw for so long!
Knowing my brother would have to live
without me. That he would be alone
in our room at night, a sheriff's badge
pinned to his chest like a silver flower
blooming above his heart.

Country Music

When the dogs in my neighborhood go wild
over the patrol car's red and blue scream, the lights hitting
someone's window like electric tickertape
and I know some of those dogs are biters
because I was someone they bit,
I begin to think about the lives of men
and how we carry the heavy load of muscle,
the rumble and ruckus, without a complaint
while vulnerability barely lifts its face from the newspaper.
But I've been drinking. I'm a little messed up
and there's something about cigars and bourbon I no longer want
to be a part of. I remember how Kate would slip out
of her jeans, her bra. How she appled my body;
all that sweet skin and core, the full mouth and pulp.
She was like a country song
playing underneath an Egyptian cotton sheet, the easy kindness
of her body finding its way into mine.
But I have a father somewhere. I have a way
I'm supposed to walk down the street like a violent decision
that hasn't been made yet.
I don't care how many hours you put in
weeding the garden
or how much you love modern dance. You'll still slip back
into your knuckles.
You can carry your groceries home
in your public radio tote bag.
You can join a book club.
You can date an Indonesian hippie with dreadlocks

but you are never far from breaking someone's jaw.
When I was twenty-three I went to a party,
drank two Coronas, and slapped my girlfriend across the face.
I wanted someone to beat me.
I wanted to get thrown into the traffic
I had made of my life,
to go crashing into the couch
where two skater kids were smoking pot out of a Pepsi can,
showing off their cuts and bruises,
talking about a friend
who ollied over a parked car
the same day he got stabbed at the mall.

Grief

When grief comes to you as a purple gorilla
you must count yourself lucky.
You must offer her what's left
of your dinner, the book you were trying to finish
you must put aside
and make her a place to sit at the foot of your bed,
her eyes moving from the clock
to the television and back again.
I am not afraid. She has been here before
and now I can recognize her gait
as she approaches the house.
Some nights, when I know she's coming,
I unlock the door, lie down on my back,
and count her steps
from the street to the porch.
Tonight she brings a pencil and a ream of paper,
tells me to write down
everyone I have ever known
and we separate them between the living and the dead
so she can pick each name at random.
I play her favorite Willie Nelson album
because she misses Texas
but I don't ask why.
She hums a little,
the way my brother does when he gardens.
We sit for an hour
while she tells me how unreasonable I've been,
crying in the check-out line,

refusing to eat, refusing to shower,
all the smoking and all the drinking.
Eventually she puts one of her heavy
purple arms around me, leans
her head against mine,
and all of a sudden things are feeling romantic.
So I tell her,
things are feeling romantic.
She pulls another name, this time
from the dead
and turns to me in that way that parents do
so you feel embarrassed or ashamed of something.
Romantic? She says,
reading the name out loud, slowly
so I am aware of each syllable
wrapping around the bones like new muscle,
the sound of that person's body
and how reckless it is,
how careless that his name is in one pile and not the other.

Trouble

Marilyn Monroe took all her sleeping pills
to bed when she was thirty-six and Marlon Brando's daughter
hung in the Tahitian living room
of her mother's house
while Stanley Adams shot himself in the head. Sometimes
you can look at the clouds or the trees
and they look nothing like clouds or trees or the sky or the ground.
The performance artist Kathy Change
set herself on fire while Bing Crosby's sons shot themselves
out of the music industry forever.
I sometimes wonder about the inner lives of polar bears. The French
philosopher, Gilles Deleuze, jumped
from an apartment window into the world
and then out of it. Peg Entwistle, an actress with no lead
roles leapt off the H in the HOLLYWOOD sign
when everything looked black and white
and David O. Selznick was king, circa 1933. Ernest Hemingway
put a shotgun to his head in a tree house
while his granddaughter, a model and actress, climbed the family tree
and overdosed on Phenobarbital. My brother opened
thirteen Fentanyl patches and stuck them on his body
until it wasn't his body anymore. I like
the way geese sound above the river. I like
the little soaps you find in hotel bathrooms because they're beautiful.
Sara Kane hung herself, Harold Pinter
brought her roses when she was still alive
and Louis Lingg, the German anarchist, lit a stick of dynamite
in his own mouth

though it took six hours for him
to die, 1887. Ludwig II of Bavaria drowned
and so did Hart Crane, John Berryman, and Virginia Woolf. If you are
traveling, you should always bring a book to read, especially
on a train. Andrew Martinez, the nude activist, died
in prison, naked, a bag
around his head while in 1815 the Polish aristocrat and writer
Jan Potocki shot himself with a silver bullet.
Sara Teasdale swallowed a bottle of blues
after drawing a hot bath
in which dozens of Roman Emperors opened their veins beneath the water.
Larry Walters became famous
for flying in a Sears patio chair and forty-five helium-filled
weather balloons. He reached an altitude of 16,000 feet
and then he landed. He was a man who flew.
He shot himself in the heart. In the morning I get out of bed, I brush
my teeth, I wash my face, I get dressed in the clothes I like best.
I want to be good to myself.

Lents District

Whenever I return a fight breaks out
in the park, someone buys a lottery ticket,
steals a bottle of vodka, lights
a cigarette underneath the overpass.
205 rips the neighborhood in half
the way the Willamette rips the city in half.
It sounds like the ocean
if I am sitting alone in the backyard
looking up at the lilac.
This is where white kids lived
and listened to Black Sabbath
while they beat the shit out of each other
for bragging rights,
running in packs, carrying baseball bats
that were cut from the same trees
our parents had planted
before the Asian kids moved in
to run the mini-marts
and carry knives to school, before the Mexicans
moved in and mowed everyone's front yard—
white kids wanting anything
anybody ever took from them in shaved heads
and combat boots.
On the weekend our furious mothers
applied their lipstick
that left red cuts on the ends of their Marlboro Reds
and our fathers quietly did whatever
fathers do

when trying to keep the dogs of sorrow
from tearing them limb from limb.
Lents, I have been away so long
I imagine that you're a musical
some rich kid from New York wrote about debt,
then threw in Kool-Aid
to make it funny. I can see the dance line,
the high kicks of the skinheads, twirling
metal pipes, stomping in unison
while the committed rage of the Gypsy Jokers
square off with the committed rage
of the single mothers.
In the end someone gets evicted, someone
gets jumped into his new family
and they call themselves Los Brazos,
King Cobras, South-Side White Pride.
Dear Lents, dear 82nd avenue, dear 92nd and Foster,
I am your strange son.
You saved me when I needed saving,
your arms wrapped around
my bassinet like patrol cars wrapped around
the school yard
the night Jason went crazy—
waving his father's gun above his head,
bathed in red and blue flashing lights,
all-American, broken in half and beautiful.

Part Three

We Are Not Temples

My friend, a Buddhist, tells me
that life is constantly changing
and that my struggle against it
is the cause of all my suffering. That and wanting
what I do not have, being less than excited about what I do,
and the shaky delusions
of an invented reality in which I probably live
most of my days. She's right.
Life changes. The sacred becomes, after many years, secular
and then turns back around as if it has forgotten its keys,
becoming sacred all over again.
It's like Florida when it was wild and native,
eventually cut down, agglomerated
with turkey-skinned, sun-burned Europeans.
Tropical diseases running willy-nilly through everyone's veins
until, once upon a time, Mr. Walt Disney
or Mr. Walt Disney's children built their castles
and tea-cup rides, making a trip to Florida almost as sacramental
as it was commercial. I'm the same way,
depending on who's loving me
or hating me, taking my letters and burning them,
ripping them up, throwing them in the air
above a bed we might have shared
while a friend cheers her on, yelling *that's right—you go girl*!
And it is right, necessary even, fuck—if I was there
listening to the Indigo Girls and drinking Chardonnay
I'd rip my letters up too. As for the invented reality
I live in, my friend is also correct. I am so much bigger

than in real life. I've played lead guitar
for famous bands, I've played lead roles
in famous movies, I've been in outer space and I've been a pig
farmer with a beautiful wife from Ireland.
But those, perhaps, are not delusions as much as they are dreams.
Not so much Florida without Disney World,
its five-dollar soft drinks and coked-out Donald Ducks
posing with five hundred sticky kids
but Florida with Seminole Indians and Sun Dances.
As far as delusions go
it must be the ones I have about kindness,
that I am never mean or have never wanted to disgrace
your wife in the coat room of a community theater.
Or that I would always give up my seat
on the bus for the elderly woman who grumbles
about how much she hates Mexicans,
that I move so that others can be more free,
that my body is a temple,
a kind of Taj Mahal or Mall of America,
were people come to pray
and spend money, where I put the wholesome
offerings of high fructose corn syrup
and carcinogens onto the altars of the lung and liver,
that I never wanted what my cousins have, their completeness
and money. Their beauty. Things like that.
Small things. Big things.
This must be why my Buddhist friend is concerned,
as she smokes her American Spirit
cigarettes. Which is not to say she's a hypocrite
or delusional
or is in any way linked to the suffering
of Native Americans,

though it might be some peculiar destiny
that one people would be dying of alcoholism
while the other succumbs to lung cancer, what it is,
as the blue smoke exhales from her small chest
which is covered, this evening, in a creamy silk top
with spaghetti straps, what it is is that we are not temples,
our bodies, no matter how many worms
work all night to make a sexy, creamy silk top
with spaghetti straps, a kind of industrial workmanship
outdone, by the way,
only through the greater exertion
of the twelve-year-old Taiwanese
who put the damn things together. No, our bodies are chemical,
organic bed and breakfasts, where we stay out too late on the beaches
of our desires and in the morning over a plate of scrambled eggs
and a hot cup of caffeine-enriched coffee,
we come running into the Shangri-la that is sober advice.
Or we meet in a bar like this one with our sacred prayer beads
in one hand and the now secular tobacco
in the other, inhaling it,
and then letting it exhale slowly like the long breath
those first men and women from Cheap End must have taken
when they walked off the plank of their Dickensian ships
and onto the sands of the untouched, divine, and humid Floridian coast.

American Standard

I have spent many hours, sitting
on the toilet, reading books by incredible people
like Mark Twain and Truman
Capote, books about strangers coming to town
and books about a boy, packing
up his belongings into a knapsack,
hopping a train, and eventually becoming a stranger himself.
I have read newspapers
and not just the comics but the metro section
with all its gore and local scandal
like the DNA of the city spinning in long columns.
I have finished whole magazines
where you can barely see the clothes for all the curving bodies.
I have been on my knees
with the stomach flu, staring into the toilet
like some people will drive to the ocean and stare at the sea.
My toilet was manufactured
by a company called American Standard and I have thrown up
more than once, looking at the blue stamp above
the lid and thinking
no one will believe me:
the American Standard taking whatever
you give it, flushing, then filling back up with water.
Standing beside the toilet
I have talked friends down
from bad acid trips, and once,
while flossing my teeth, experienced
a deep sorrow lost forever in the mirror.
All in a bathroom! And that's not all.

There's a woman standing inside the bathroom,
against the door, which is unlocked,
and I am standing against her
and the party outside is standing against the walls of the house
and she is engaged to a nice man
from Colorado and I am lifting up her dress
with my teeth. No one gets her like the dress gets her
and that is why men want to pull it off.
It's jealousy. It's moving in on the conversation she's been having
with the fabric all night
and that conversation, the one you are
not a part of, is getting hot and heavy
so now there are half-moons of sweat appearing
beneath each breast and maybe
that is why you end up in the bathroom
next to a toilet with a candle on top,
a handful of her hair,
and her head reaching back
toward two shoulder blades that have been scratched by her fiancé
the night they fought about whatever it is
people fight about so that later they can throw each other around
without their clothes on. I have her underwear off now
and now she is sort of half-sitting on the edge of the sink
and I'm reaching for the door
because when she pulls me out of my jeans
I decide to lock it. I hear it click
and then I hear someone knocking, yelling
hurry up! but I don't want to hurry up
so I start thinking about the time
I almost went to Africa
and how I imagined Ethiopia
was going to be, and how the people there
were probably the kindest people on earth.

The Cows of Point Reyes

Because Laura was driving I was free
to take pictures of the cows who looked so close
when I pushed down my index finger, making the camera
click. Those slow giants, I thought
they'd come out glossy and huge like the tasteless
strawberries people grow in California,
but they didn't, they came out small like the wild ones
in Oregon, in someone's backyard
next to the tomato and rosemary.
This was along the coast, the cows with their souls
mooing away in their hearts
like the wind in old westerns
you might have seen when you were young and it forever shook
you to tears or made you love
someone you'd never known. Those big-hearted cows,
black and white gods chewing the grass
of America, making milk or making meat
I don't know which, but making something there
on the hillside. I was looking out
toward the ocean where the whales were hiding, orbiting
along some aquatic jet-stream like dark planets,
and I was looking into the rear-view mirror as well,
where Laura's eyes were looking at me, both of us
so close to the cows and the sea
at the same time, reminding me
of an India I read about
where kindness is called *Ahimsa*
though it could be something else, something like a red balloon

or an open hand. I often take pictures of people or animals
so when they're gone I can remind myself
that they're real, that I have proven the unprovable fact
that not only do I have a heart
but it grows like a sentimental chrysanthemum
my parents planted in the seventies
while their friends were flying helicopters over what was left
of Saigon. I don't know why
I miss the cows so deeply, why
when I look at the picture and they appear so small
I want to cry. Loss is a funny thing to feel
when you never knew the thing you miss. But I suppose
I loved the cows, my irrational heart
blowing open the doors of the schmaltzy saloon
where my feelings stay up late
drinking scotch, listening to old punk records,
which aren't even old
in the fossil-universe-space-station we live in.
Maybe it was Laura making everything
sublime with her red hair doing crazy things, the window
rolled down, the salt in the air.
The night before we had driven down a little road
with the stars and the fences
and I knew I was living my life
there in the car, looking out
but not knowing if it was the ocean or the hills.
Sometimes, when you're driving in the dark,
you can be anywhere, you can turn
the headlights off and bend toward hope and happiness and the good
stuff about death. Death! My favorite kind
of fear. I think about it whenever I fly
and whenever something good happens I give it a little kiss.

If I were more like the cows
it wouldn't matter. But it's good to be human and have
a little fear tucked away in some corner of my body,
in the orange bathtub at the B&B
where I had death hiding in my left hand,
where I brought the washcloth up
and felt the water running down her shoulders,
burning a candle in the room
and Laura in or out of her clothes.
I had never thought about the life
expectancy of cows or how they would make me feel
Elysian, that they would mean so much,
that I would even suffer
because of my great feelings for them or that I would dream about Laura
the night I came home, and in it
she would be sitting near me in a theater where we had gone to see
a movie about Sweden we both loved in different ways.

Chick Corea is Alive and Well!

Which makes the elegy I wrote for him seem a little distasteful.
Let me tell you, just because you see someone in a black
and white photograph doesn't mean he's dead.
Even if you find the photograph in an old-looking
box inside your grandmother's closet,
the person in it standing against an old Ford
with a goat walking past and a farm in the distance,
he may still be alive, in a nursing home being fed
by a large Kentuckian named Tony, but alive
all the same. And it's the same with people
much older than you. Just because
they were buying cups of coffee
for a nickel and listening to Sarah Vaughan live
at the Blue Note, they're not always sleeping
through their hangovers under a quiet blade of grass
in God's Acre. When I bought the Chick Corea album
and saw him in the silvery sheen of the cover art,
smoking an unfiltered cigarette, the smoke rising
over his face like the hem of a silk dress,
I didn't even blink. He was dead. And I? I was sad,
listening to his fingers, his poor dead fingers, flying
like ghosts over IT DON'T MEAN A THING
IF IT AIN'T GOT THAT SWING, and thinking
this man's a genius! playing Ellington like a bartender
plays a Singapore Sling, all that maraschino cherry
sweetness, a little clink of ice, and his voice
doing a kind of mumble-moan
over the keys like a man whose been raised

from the dead, looking down at a woman's knees
after years in the dirt, singing yeaahh!

yeaahh! this is what I'm talkin' about, yeaahh! this good, sweet life!

American Studies

There's an artist that lives nearby
whose life, she says, is her art.
And to that unbearably self-conscious
bon mot she is willing to have love affairs with anyone
willing, themselves, to be a living, breathing,
piece of art. Love letters or telephone calls. I suppose
you could do anything, drive her out
of town and take her in the backseat, her left foot
raised high and pressing
against the window, her right foot shuffling on the floorboard.
You could also watch her make art
by herself on a bed
in some hotel. Sitting there in the dark
like you were in some strange theater of the avant-garde.
I'm thinking about that guy in New York
who stood on stage in an old meat packing warehouse,
the audience full of the very young
and painful, waiting for this "happening" to happen,
when the artist, standing
beneath a single lightbulb, pulls out a gun and shoots himself
in the foot. Well, Ralph Stanley says,
cheer up my brothers, live in the sunshine, we'll understand
it all by and by. And by and by
we do. Sometimes love gets commissioned
and sometimes art shoots itself in the foot. At least it's art.
At least it's not some grassy knoll bullshit
or some teenager walking into the cafeteria with a sawed-off
and an overcoat. Cheer up

my brothers, our Master is sleeping it off in heaven.
He is waiting for his children, his tired,
his poor, his huddled masses. He's looking
for an artist he likes. I like Victor Maldonado. I like his painting
of the boy in a dunce hat reading to a circus bear.
Victor's from Mexico. He paints
drop-top cadillacs, police dogs, the legs of little girls, and helicopters.
Everybody loves his canvas
of Coca-Cola cans and McDonald's french fries. Hey
remember when they were freedom fries?
Wasn't that a minute ago? Wasn't that, for Christ's sake,
a little indignant?
And speaking of Christ,
we have Christ in a jar of urine, the artist of which
was not dragged into a van, his teeth
kicked out, his body left hanging from a streetlight. We can
make anything we want. It's awesome.
Like Justin Richel's painting of George Washington,
lying on his death bed,
an arch of blood, a spout bending over one slave and into the bowl
of another. He paints our forefathers
in beehive wigs with actual bees coming out.
Whole wigs made out of cakes
and pies. He's a good artist. He's skinny and worked
for his father mixing cement, putting in drywall,
then going home and making
little portraits of Paul Revere, Thomas Jefferson,
Thomas Paine, you name it.
Little portraits with moving parts like eyes and tongues. Jefferson's
tongue moving in and out, some woman,
some slave on his mind,
making it burn and shuck and jive. In the dining hall

of the artists' residency, an artist
places a sign on each of the tables that reads
"Niggers Only." Everyone sits down and blushes,
gets pissed off and self-referential,
saying I didn't do this. This isn't
my work. That's art
slapping the baby and making it cry.
I'd like to do something with sticks. Maybe make them
into a house or something. Maybe have you bend me over
your knee and beat me. We could
call it "I Never Had a Father"
and people would get to thinking about it.
You could dress up
in a powdered wig with top hat, white gloves, white paint
smeared over your face,
a dinner jacket with tails. The whole bit.
While I beg and beg
and call you boss, my little superpower.

Lucky Number

I am betting all of it tonight,
whatever that may be,
on the locust and the amber
bugs I can't even name
but love the way we love children
with a cache of forgiveness
and humor, stumbling
through the playground in yellow
rainboots and Band-Aids.
I am putting down my chips
for the starling
because she sang me out of my hangover
and I am letting my dice roll
on the mole
who wore glasses in my childhood
and wrapped himself up
in a blanket, near the fire he made,
in the tiny house
beneath the roots of an evergreen.
I am betting my winnings
on a friend I was unfaithful to.
I am leaving the blue ribbons
of my dishonesty
around the doorknobs of women
who would have been better off
without the impersonations
of famous operas
I played out on single, full, and queen

sized beds. I want this lucky
number to hit
so I can look the palm tree in his shaggy face.
I am willing to break the bank
for the geese, walking along the river's edge
like thugs in white overalls,
I am willing to spend my final dollar
on a twenty to one
that the Golden Retriever I saw last night
will win by a nose, just enough
to walk awhile with redemption.
Some mud on my shoes, a little blood on my clothes.

Poem for the Night Emily Opened Her Beer with a Bic Lighter

In Vermont there are maple trees and bears and log cabins
and a university or two
where people are learning about right angles
and the philosophy of Kant.
It's also the magisterial home of the moon
which seems to cut and lilt
through every branch and over every peak. I sat below it
on the steps of an old church
converted into a lecture hall, no longer
the house of God, no longer the property of souls
who prayed and sang and felt bad
about all the bad things they had done.
It was night time. It was no longer a church.
Emily opened her beer with a Bic lighter. Sitting there
I could hear the river
and it made me feel important. More important, I imagine,
than Emily felt when she finally finessed
the right amount of pressure
between the cap of the beer and the chewed-up
end of the lighter, popping the cap
into her lap, the river, moving in its one direction,
made me feel as if I was living
the same way, with the same purpose, and by proxy
had the same power, the same
hydro-ecstatic-willingness not to be exhausted
by my own body. The river ran near my room
and I listened to it every night.
I kept my window open. I kept my shoes lined against the wall.
When I'm drinking beer I like to stare into the fire

a friend has built out of kindling and dry logs, some news
paper helping it burn, looking blankly forward
at the flames, my face looking absolutely surprised
as if someone I never imagined
were to pull their jeans off
and I am slipping my hands through them,
helping them over the ankles.
I helped Emily's over her ankles
the night she opened her beer with a Bic lighter
because I liked her, and I liked the part about her knees
and the part about her wrists.
I liked the line about her breasts, the humming
her nipples made
and the double entendre in her mouth.
I liked the well-written starlight when she blinked
and the page-turning,
oh-hell-yes, when she breathed.
I liked the one about her ass and the one about her neck.
My favorite might have been her shoulders,
her skin glowing
like some deep tenderness that had surfaced for a moment.
Tenderness and beer go well together.
In fact, just last weekend, Delmore Schwartz, who is dead,
was telling me, *My tendency*
is tenderness, he was saying, *I'm naturally affectionate.*
If he wanted to he could have
opened a beer with his teeth,
sitting in Vermont, the Green Mountains rising up
behind him like this immense dream
I am having about the largesse of life, sitting
on the steps of a church-gone-lecture hall
with Emily and a six-pack of beer.

The Small Clasp

Your breasts were two drunken parents
coaching little league practice
but smaller, I remember, than the disappointment
parents wrap around children
and now they have been replaced by others.
Some were like exposed negatives,
two copies of a Maria Callas biography,
a pair of Dutch clogs,
two pieces of chocolate cake
that left me thirsty for two glasses of milk,
pierced, tattooed, each different,
even from each other;
one always seeming a little brighter,
a little larger or smaller
at midday or midnight, while it rained
or began to snow, sticking to the sidewalk.
I remember my friend's wife
the night I lifted her shirt
over her shoulders
in the tiny upstairs bathroom
while he argued about Eliot
and the Jews with the woman
I would eventually drive home.
Honor will only carry you so far
before it drops you on your ass.
You can't run from it
but you can get close, standing out in the cold,
lighting your little cigar, talking

a woman's ear off. Making her feel
lonelier with every story you tell.
I have learned to conquer loneliness
the way television conquers loneliness.
The woman in the car commercial, bending
over the hood, her breasts telling me
this is the car for you, handsome.
You have to believe in it
if you want to survive. You have to
let the old lies into bed and make them sing for you.
And it's the same thing when I dream
about your breasts and a floating riding crop.
I have to remember how wonderful it feels, pulling
my hands out of my pockets, moving
them slowly between someone's spine
and yellow t-shirt, happy to unhook the small clasp
without the fingerprints of love,
without the familiar sound of our neighbors fighting
and all the effortless moaning that went with you.

The World is Too Huge to Grasp

Still, tiger, there's no reason
not to tie your wife up
if that's what she's been dreaming about
in traffic. No reason not to
go out and eat twenty doughnuts
if that's what you want instead of granola
because, whether you like it or not,
it's a skeleton you're wearing
under those Italian jeans. For my part
I'm going to watch hours of television
wearing nothing but a pair of running shoes.
I'm going to walk out
into the yard and begin courting
the rosebushes. I'm not going to
let a little thing like the world stand in my way.
Why should I? I understand it
as much as I understand penguins
and I still go to the zoo. I still watch them
swimming underwater.
It's like watching really beautiful gods
moving within a universe
that other, taller gods built for them
out of compassion and ingenuity.
It would be easy to sit at the bar smoking,
drinking, ruminating about the why of penguins,
pulling our hair out, crying into our gin
about how the penguins have forsaken us,
how nature is having another party
and we're not invited.

I like the world in all its incredible forms.
When I've had the shit beat out of me, my friends
who have died their violent and accidental
deaths, falling from windows, swerving
into the lights of traffic, my suffering,
my unearned joy, my hand reaching up
through the yards of fabric that made your dress,
the midnight movies, all the kids huffing
all the paint thinners, the comedy
of the poor and the ruthlessness
of the rich, how we're too hungry to fight,
too crushed by debt and the psycho
promise of there's-always-tomorrow,
of rent-to-own, the smell
of carrots, the smell of gasoline, the mysteries
of bread and wine, the sky
in Montana with Laura beneath it,
the sky in Portland when my brother was buried
in his little tin of ash, the happiness
of love and the pity of sex, the bathroom stalls,
the fruit markets, Rob proposing on one knee
wearing a panda costume, sweating inside
the fake fur, his bride in love,
the quarterback's son
paralyzed from the neck down
and then gone, the fear and fetish
of genitals, the way
we beat our selves into our suits and high heels.
I see how we are with each other.
I see how we act. It's not the world
with its ten-zillion things we should be grasping.
but the sincerity of penguins, the mess we made of the roses.

Notes

"The Black Album"

The line "I don't know, now, if any of us get out of this." is from David Rivard's poem "Acceptance."

"All-American Poem"

The phrase "one broken heart deserves a heart that has been differently broken" is from Kenneth Koch's poem "A Study in Time."

The line "I love you but I'm turning to my verses and my heart is closing like a fist" is from Frank O'Hara's poem "Mayakovsky."